If Food Grew On TREES

by Krista Tarasyuk

Inspired by the idea of planting food bearing foliage along sidewalks instead of decorative foliage.

Written and illustrated by
Krista Tarasyuk

What a fine world we would have
If food grew on trees;

If water fell from the sky;
If the ground sprouted seeds.

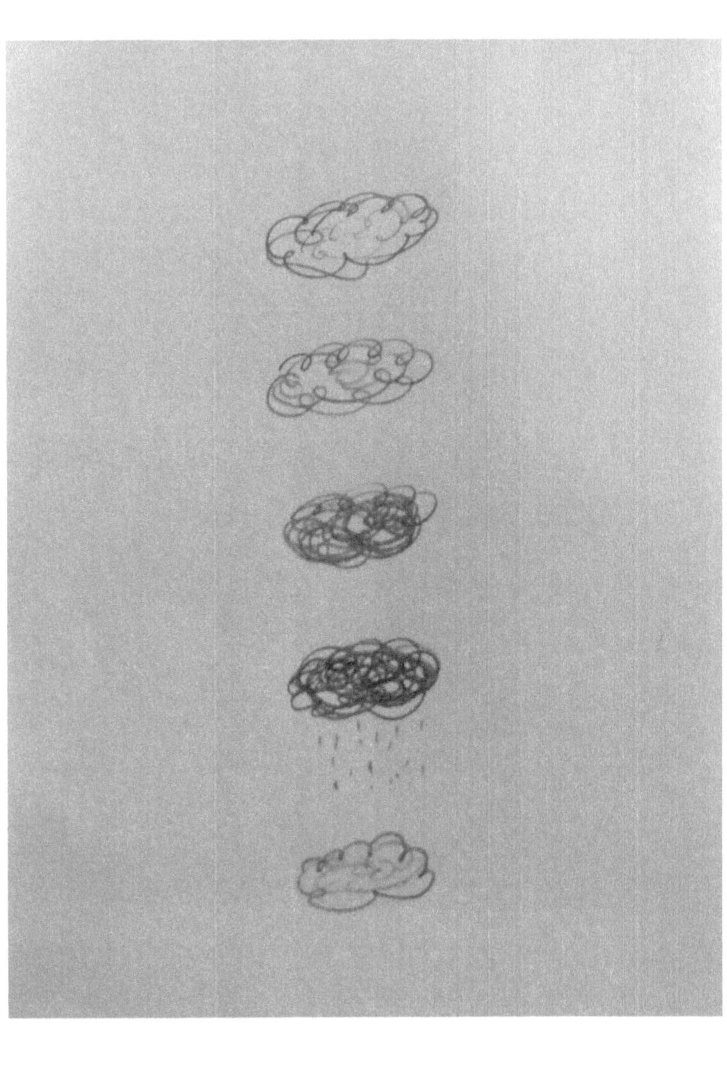

What a fine world we would have
If no one ever felt hunger;

If no one ever felt thirst;
If humans and Earth helped each
other.

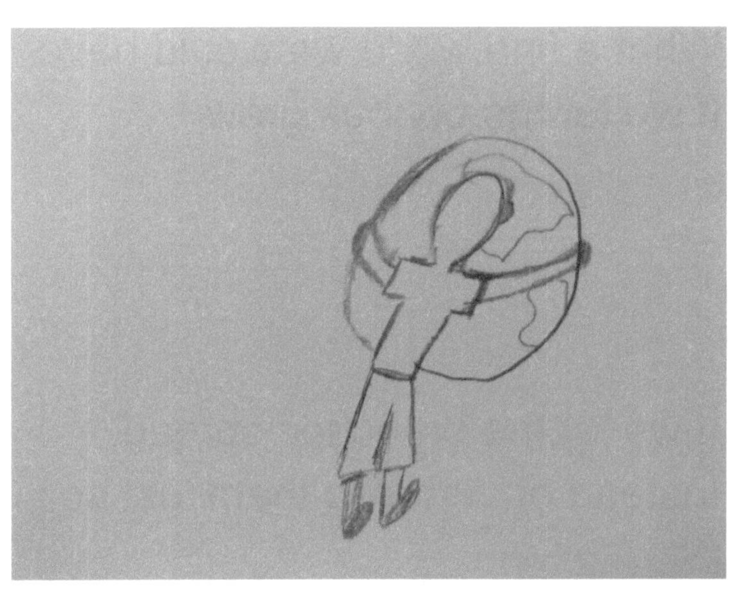

What a fine world we would have
If we let the bushes grow;

If we let the branches spread,
Instead of trimming them just so.

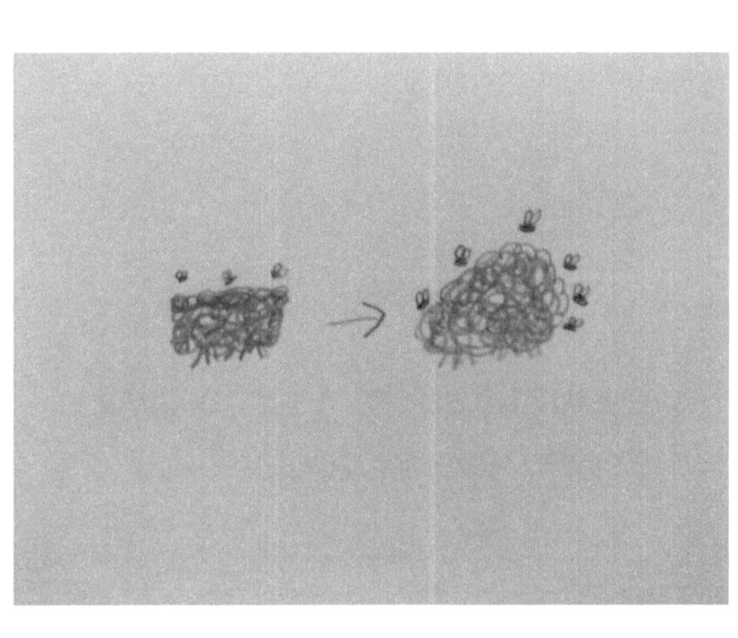

What a fine world we would have
If we had enough food to share;

If we taught each other to give
What we have to spare.

What a fine world we would have
If the plants weren't so pretty,

But berry bushes and apple trees
Lined streets along every city.

What a fine world we would have
If food lined each busy street;

If there was shade on the
sidewalk;
If every pedestrian could eat.

= Food

What a fine world we would have
If we embraced Earth's ways;

If we carried an umbrella upside
down;
If we collected the rain on rainy
days.

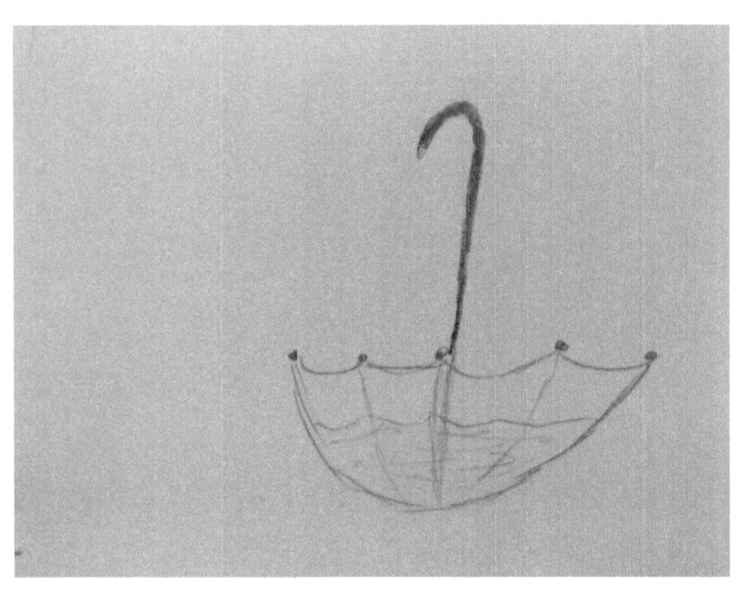

What a fine world we would have
If we just took a minute each day

To listen to Earth and each other
And listen to what they say.

What a fine world we would have
If food grew on trees;

If water fell from the sky;
If the ground sprouted seeds.

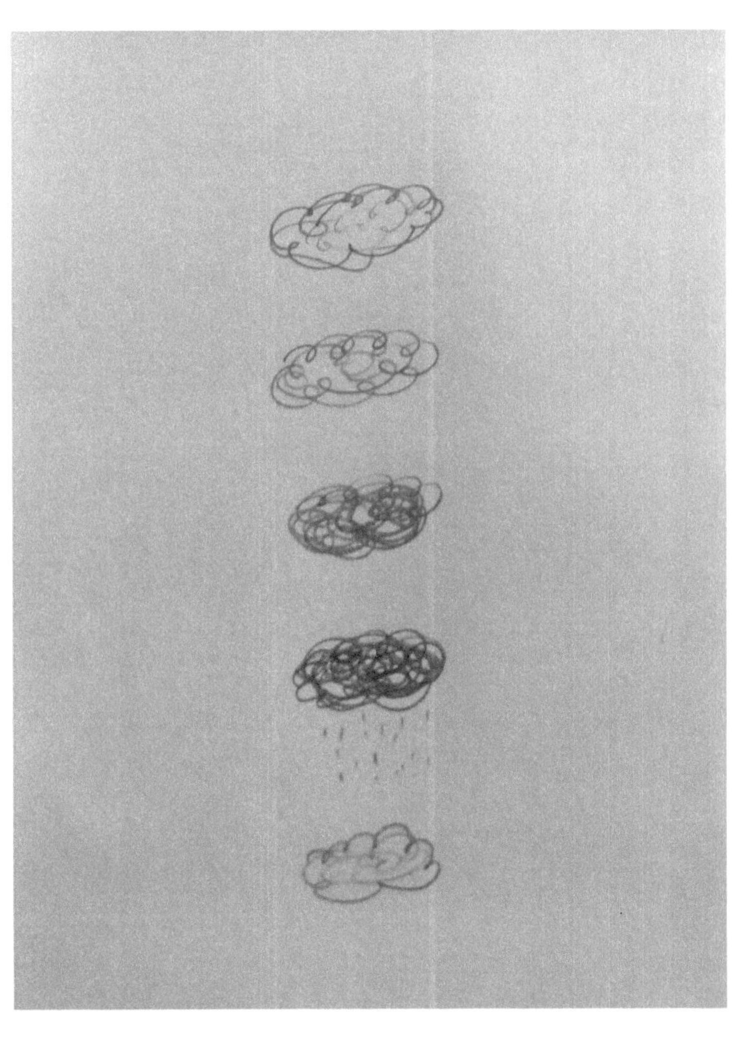

It does.

www.ingramcontent.com/pod-product-compliance
Lightning Source LLC
Chambersburg PA
CBHW020948160726
47993CB00007B/2997